ALL WRONG HORSES ON FIRE

THAT GO AWAY IN THE RAIN

all wrong horses on fire that go away in the rain

SARAIN FRANK SOONIAS

NeWest Press

Library and Archives Canada Cataloguing in Publication
Title: All wrong horses on fire that go away in the rain : poems / Sarain Frank Soonias.
Names: Soonias, Sarain Frank, author.
Series: Crow said poetry.
Description: Series statement: Crow said poetry
Identifiers: Canadiana (print) 20240464494 | Canadiana (ebook) 20240464710 | ISBN 9781774391143 (softcover) | ISBN 9781774391150 (EPUB)
Subjects: LCGFT: Poetry.
Classification: LCC PS8637.O66 A79 2025 | DDC C811/.6—dc23

NeWest Press wishes to acknowledge that the land on which we operate is Treaty 6 territory and Métis Nation of Alberta Region 4, a traditional meeting ground and home for many Indigenous Peoples, including Cree, Saulteaux, Niitsitapi (Blackfoot), Métis, Dene, and Nakota Sioux, since time immemorial.

Editor: Claire Kelly
Editor for the Press: Jennifer Bowering Delisle
Cover and interior design: Natalie Olsen, Kisscut Design

 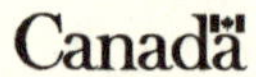

NeWest Press acknowledges the support of the Canada Council for the Arts, the Government of Alberta through the Ministry of Arts, Culture and Status of Women and the Edmonton Arts Council for support of our publishing program. We acknowledge the financial support of the Government of Canada through the Canada Book Fund for our publishing activities.

NeWest Press
#201, 8540-109 Street
Edmonton, Alberta   T6G 1E6
NeWest Press   www.newestpress.com

No bison were harmed in the making of this book.
Printed and bound in Canada
1 2 3 4 25 26 27 28

For Ring and Doris, Frank and Bertie

Don't break the circle before the song is over.
Because all of our people. Even the ones long
gone. Are holding hands.

Sarain Stump

Myth served as a story in which people could
connect themselves to the past. And thereby
connect themselves to the present and the
future. They just speak to some lame notions
about the past. But they don't connect with
anything. We've lost touch with the essence
of myth.

Sam Shepard

Seemed easier than just waitin' around to die.

Townes Van Zandt

i need help. i'm not saying i'm suicidal
but i'm not not saying i'm suicidal.

—Sunrise Medical Center, Vancouver, BC.
January 24, 2020

week one

MIKISIW-WACÎK

harvest and grow
breathe and recover
some lack of control
all perfect

words not mine
heartbeat shared

    my reason
        my reason
            my reason

a spectre invited to the party

great belly laughs of forgiveness

lost son,
        welcome home

week two

1638

the memories

burned

in a wildfire

about-face men

this is your blind eye

mine is a child

reborn of fire

scroll upon scroll

birchbark crackling

eastern woodlands

1638

i don't forget

i can't

RANDY

you've done wrong, my friend
you are facing misdeeds
mind my tone
i'm used to needing control

        don't rush
        bears know salmon
                know rebirth

        you'll lope
       you will lose fights
        you'll fear fear
                and you will expand
                      you'll leave much behind

he'll explain as you go
they see it coming
            be still now

babies do not launch until an ageless voice tells them so
someday in a land with colours unlike this

the goal
        to strive
      cannot be of your mind
            aim your bow in our starlands   and let go

you cannot know the trajectory

GHOST OF ANOTHER

being born
where am i going to
suddenly i knew
was afraid to tell

i wish i can not be lost
found now
bad fire all around
waiting for us to heal

she throws salt in the wind
still a mystery
        my earth
            my wind
                my mother

OKÂWÎMÂ

my road is a long one, dear mother
i want to see what you see
just a moment

a boy is just a boy
his mother is the mystery

she goes fearlessly through the world
    she trembles in her boots
        she would love
            and she would kill

her road is a hard one

IT'S NOT MY HOME

it's all inside us
                believe your cousin, you stupid boy
lessons in the least of creatures, sickness in the strongest

why not hide together,
              flee together,
                    stay strong for each other?
                          deny these cruel dogs that never stop eating

let go and come back

                    this answer inside—
why hide? why hide?
              your teacher is my teacher
                    your god is my god

the inverse is an old kitchen table
ashtray soot where i take off and dream
two men circle the issue inside my head
no one tells the truth
i bled and died
alone in a burned-out basement
i forgot existed

there is a path of green
and we unbridled for a moment

the older cousins are mustangs and they prance in the sun
but i turn back
it is what i know
i know what is at the bottom of the well

quiet sloughs and long driveways
turn the world on its axis, child
you are cold black coffee in an urn
that hears voices from another time

mosom and nohkom minding the baby
you'll never stop crying for them
but i love you, my boy
    you are free
        forgive me
            i am here now

some know where ghosts are

YOUR COUNTERPART

seems to be in hell
                    fire-caked liquid pain
            and the evil unleashed
            from another land
the boy on fire

MISSISSIPPI IS MY BIG WATER

i had to kill

part of myself

at a young age

because the terror

        because words

                mobs

dead mother hanging on a string

NIMISHOOMIS (RANDOLPH)

i don't wanna avoid the hell i was promised
        get my hair back
                walk down to the dock

i'm new here
it's red and purple and orange and yellow

i don't need to wait on their hell anymore
        their pain and unfettered shame
                their sick wells

i think i'll stay here a while

sister delina,
                        my rock
quietly sitting strong for us

our life is their hell
        this red and orange
                and purple yellow

these old ghosts and bright babies

if you could play me as keys
in between tones,
where would the beat come from?

can you be a heaven
if the holy spirit resides in all of us?

no,
you are water
birdsong
the sound of
our babies running
in the bush
leaving prints with the other babies
who teach in the shadows
       quietly godlike
           alone and forever

please, be safe
patient longing is a boy and man
i am still in the forest
but i march now
how could you blame me?
but you would tease

and this is why all
this is why i love you

THE TREES ARE THICK (NOW I SEE YOU)

stand on a hill
and watch them march
the soulless guile
blind men
impervious to beauty

and then you see

we are the fire
    we burn and crackle
        smoulder and pop

    we are alive in the places you are not

this love of ours dormant
    no longer, my love

—

one day, my love
    one day the fighting will stop
and we will know peace

and i will not need to hold you up to the sky
because you will know how to walk along the stars

and I'll rest easy knowing the fire is still burning on the shore
the uncles' laughter carrying me off to gentle slumber

BIG MAN STRUMMING A GUITAR

the spirits have not left the stumps

the salmon burst from the water

your daughter is alive

and her life gives you life

break into song, you old rascal

yours is a good life

yours is a reason to be grateful

OLD BOOTS AND COMFY JEANS

old boots and comfy jeans   worn-in laugh lines
and maddening, happy children   short tall
unlimited sun babies   souls born of electric
moonlight and salt water spray
                                        i will not look a sea
horse in the mouth   one of them would charge
headlong off a bluff
                    chubby little seal pups learn how
crabs pinch   sand is a sibling who never sleeps
waits patiently
a racoon skirts the tree line   she has been there
before and smiles
                    "you're up early"
"well. . ." she says
                    i nod and smile back
                                        my youngest,
the mighty hunter, marches up from the edge with a
dead gull
          she ambles off to sleep some more
i run for my life

KILL THE INDIAN, SPARE THE CHILD

then a dark told me,
your child is mine

these desperate dogs scrambling after viscera
the honour   just cow shit
stamped into grooves under boots

i should kill you where you stand
                you promise me hell
but you, an army of wendigo

        no balance to your trickster
        no joy in your games
                you only bring death because you are dead
                you bob and float bob and float

                                you cannot see you're already gone

EAST VAN TERMINAL

the lead dog to my right is no sheep
    he was a guide
        he was everything
    but he was not me
        i was not him

mine is a lake beside other lakes that never dries
      mine is a prairie everlasting
      gazing beyond myself towards another

gulls caw out above the drone of the multitude
servants alive but not
cannot miss a step
    bad water
        wretched thicket
            manufactured wheels are no circle
and nothing ever springs anew

the whales pull the night over top of themselves
and your babies lose their vitality much too soon

      cannot be me
        should not be you

            the drone never stops at my feet
              the drone never stops in the air

be still
root past your prison floor
      deep into what a child knows all along

the truth buried in warm welcome gravel

THE PEOPLE ON THE SHORE LOOK TO YOU

babes born of cosmos
they are the before and after
    the gods chorus
        symphonic crescendo

rise up, you children in giants' clothing
you are not the lies you tell yourself

the father does not do bad work

smash the water with granite palms
the sting pushes against this calcified levee
    this pathetic joke of boundary
        this nonsense

alone
they can only know this alone

he was there
        go to him

the fool knows the babes were gods
    the land the mother
    the land the mother
        beyond
        beyond
          beyond

there is nothing

but they'll assure you hell
  you'll go anyway

week three

DONNIE

walk for a day around a rectangle
                    start in the morning
return at dusk

your uncle had buffalo in the pen
near where the adventure happened

                              what if you were always brave?

                                    is it still a rectangle?

there is a rectangle
and many spend
much much time in a pen
they chew
        swallow
                digest

but the buffalo are gone now

                                    who is in the pen?

there is a tall fat man
laughing above them all
        does not belong
                and smiles unnatural
                        breathes unnatural
                                dying on his feet
                                but lives forever
i'm gonna kill him

people need to get to the creek
where the adventure happened

drink and poke your nose in the water

there is a rectangle
you walk around in the hot sun
        in the hot hot sun

SPEAKING VOICE

my eyes burn   but now i see
gentle words from a soul i've never met

i want to burn   but it's time
                        to fill an expanse

truth is you do not exist
      you cannot be labelled
and you start walking—

you spiral in words
                        waves are coming
                              voices leaving

    let go
              waves
                    feel
                    trust

you won't even need to say goodbye

MAYBE I LIKE 69 BECAUSE

i don't think it ever ends   maybe i love sixty-nine because
i've been here many times   a guy's understanding of things
sure would change   maybe not the whole reason   but big
thundering dogs racing in tandem across the field breathe heavy
and strain like thoroughbreds

                                                bears bark and huff in time
like a song   and if i blink too long, things might be different
real different   my feet are on stone on grass and we can't
drink the water   i'm trying as hard as i can   but
you can't rush the tide   hell, why would you want to?

GUIDE ME WHEREVER I GO

can you feel a vision you haven't seen?

waiting for a plant to grow,
        but you already know
        the before and after

                                she is the wave

and that's okay
you can see and not explain

wait till her belly swells

        try to explain forgetting the world

snow

melts to my

right on a big hill

with captives and captors

someone said go slow and mind

impatience   i didn't listen then

sure do now   but is this another

mountain? or a gentle tremor?   this wave

never reaches shore   like a song played over

and over in an empty hall   i can see the universe

in a pond underneath rocky bluffs   where spirits roll grass

between their fingertips   i can't see you alive   alone in

in the clouds   standing atop a quiet mountain with my eyes closed

GRIEF

take me with you
i don't want to stay without you
i will wait in this place
and leave at your side

no, my son
it will be your time one day
but you need to keep going
my hands are not strong now
but i'm at your side

this loss is only a difficult dream
i'll be there when you lose
when you're scared

open your eyes
look at your boy

this is how it was supposed to be
my fire will always be burning
and you will sit with me when it's our time
go and be strong like a young man
i love you
and wait patiently every day
their love is inside you
go to it, my beautiful son
my big strong boy
your dad, always

WHAT SNOW THAT MELTS ON YOUR FACE

do you know where you'll be
in many winters?

i could tell you
could you hear?

hers is a beautiful song,
wind and rain, rocks,
and a solitary lion
on the side of a great hill

climb one day and go to her,
leave worldly noise behind

you know what snow that melts on your face
the girl

TED AND PHYLLIS

hello, old man   general supreme of this garden   your
words sway me in the breeze   may i sit with your daughter
for a moment?   just a few moments and i'll go on my way

she relaxes me   her voice could put me to sleep if i was not
so happy

          may i pour you another glass?   i want to play a
song for your daughter

               i am nervous when we speak and search
for meanings   her hair hangs softly and my hopes cascade
above the orchard

                    your wife was a brave woman   she walked
atop a bluff and faced a bear

                         beautiful old man, i'm still in love
with her   we listen to music   she has seen my tears
                                                       his
daughter sighs   she is nothing that i need and everything
that i want
               the sun sets   she is laughing and we walk in
time between the rows   a loon cries out   her mother
has killed a bear

ALL WRONG HORSES ON FIRE

i won't say his name
     bring me a child to leave on a mountain first
          bring me a village to slaughter
           a club with heft
put it in my palm
and bring me the father

they will breed ruinous children
lost, like ghosts around a family dinner

i will rip the heart from his failing chest
     and show him what loss looks like

i'll summon forgiveness
     from somewhere beyond me

          and his oily root
          will be returned to its thirsty husk
          and he will go on his way

forgiveness cannot be above us

theirs is a soul adrift in the middle of a quiet lake
     and their notion of eternity
asking for a comforting voice
  and hearing none

I CAN'T HEAR ANYTHING

i can't hear anything
but i can see everything

play my game

    be safe

there's some words that i won't say

i can't hear anything
but i can see everything

play my game

    be safe

there's some words that i won't say

    someone went and broke in me

i can't hear
but i can see

NEAR DEATH

you know those feelings, don't you?
makes your skin crawl, i bet
i didn't want anyone to know i buried it

    a crypt in wet fertile ground
a meridian always shifting

trust the visions in your eyes
and the voices in your blood
cuz it's not your breath you're gonna lose

you're gonna be easier now

    ancestors never stop loving
i don't remember an invitation
  maybe it just floats along

        waters don't just halt and it's over
          you've always known
breathe

VIBRATIONS

there are four walls in a place and i am safe   but i am
peering up from the bottom of a large pond   *ripple and
distortion*   but i can see   i can feel your words
through the *scared*   *can't you see you're fading away
into something bright and eternal?*   gotta die first, i
guess   but we are here and a buffalo is best left be
our numbers are much greater than they know
an endless rumble of thunder   lay on a hill and rest
away away away   tears will dry and come again
this cycle is love   this love is eternal   let
it ring out quietly, and watch the buffalo run to the horizon

WAVE CHILD

           she is on your beach
and you make her coffee before you start to worry
           she is an answer that changes each day
maybe every time the tide,
maybe while the moon and stars
  and her beautiful soft belly
                  rise and fall in unison
                     fulfilled in cosmic rhythm
did she ever really change?
      maybe she was always meant to be seasons
knowing waves receding flush across eager sand and rocks
that busied a bloodline forgotten
      and always present

      she has never changed and is change
running her nails across your chest   wake up
  you know riches that are rain-burst from birthing clouds
  and rivers and oceans that rise again,

perfect circle within,
with or without you

stumble headlong into a spring that will never cease

lay naked in the sand and speak to her
                she does not yield
                she does not end

                    keep going
       and know she always is

week four

NANCY

i)

there is a cabin on the shore
amidst the dark trees
          where i'll go again in time

there is a loon in the bay
      and a rock at the point
              guiding us
                  and always will be

ii)

i have cousins
i laugh with baby muskrats
they grow when i'm not looking

iii)

or when i'm gone

iv)

tethered to the same rock
until our fire catches
somewhere new

v)

        there is a shoreline
        that goes on forever

where you walk
and walk
with loved ones
and never tire

vi)

rocks shift underfoot

vii)

but one cousin, nancy,
i see her always
on the shoreline
smiling
amidst the dark trees

OSCANA KASASTEKI

then the water came rushing down
and the valley was all death

some could not be held back
     the roots that tether
             the ones who know that
i would be an eagle child
and tell you
what i saw
when paskwaw mostos
came from the water
     grunting
          chuffing
the gift would be shirked by others

you cannot always know

keep breathing well

THIS IS TOO MUCH

you're gonna be a beautiful grandma
don't sigh
my love appreciates
i mean
i look into the mirror
there's change now

i think we just gotta stick with it
there's gonna be loss
and we'll lose each other at times

i miss you already
but i will stick with it
and i know that you will

i was in love with beautiful singers when i started writing
they sounded like lamp light
and the saddest girls
and warriors who wouldn't advertise being the strongest
now all i want is you to talk
just speak

everything i do is for us
        and for them
                and maybe i'll get lucky
                        and they'll sound just like you
but not too soon
hopefully down the road
but not too soon

CURIOSITY

oh, hello sirens
like looking across fifteen yards of river
moving just a little too fast
maybe this is the lighter side
there's no cap on your dance
dreams were never supposed to be governed

old men in pain make jokes
and look at you a little sideways through one good eye
whisper their honey goodnight
and wake up alone every morning

the other half of the world is a chorus
of tantalizing flowers you cannot name
and who needs to?

the happiest kids make their own rules
based on single-minded want and need

i need to walk again
but the grass sure is green
and the kids seem happy,
if not a little bossy

QUAZANCE (THERE IS A WOMAN AND SHE KNOWS BEST)

there is a bear who lolls up and down the cutbank
there are stars and planets i could never shake
orbiting me when i sleep

when i open my eyes
        and an old woman sits, and tells me
you've always known, haven't you
        she will laugh
                she will smile
                        and she will help you forget

and you will start again

there is a bear in the stars
and an old woman who has seen
she will laugh
she will smile
and you will start again

GIIZHIG

no,
don't talk to me
we know everything we need to know

i take up the first damning steps
somewhere i was young running in the sand
and I knew I would be back
because always the waves
but now i could not hear them

slowly falling upward

dad was taking a walk to look for water
mum was throwing the ball
   and we leapt and strained
         and she didn't tell us to mind our knees
               and when jess dove and got dirty
then mum said a bug flew in her eyes
because she said her eyes have bug magnets
and she got some kleenex

sometimes i'm sad
but dad gets us up early to run or shovel
or sometimes he lets us try a sip of his coffee
and then we play tag and wake up in the sand
and dad calls us wacask

he's a good dad
i don't feel sad around him
he says if i wanna learn
the land will always teach me

JOSSY

there are little people
asleep under the rock   *i went away*
holding little hands
in a circle   *to die myself*
where all different
men cannot go   *alone*
the little footsteps
skipping along a
gravel road   *under red dusty*
between an orange   *rocks*
school and a sacred
place   *i could not throw*
just the wind   *the ball*
rustling
through brittle leaves   *and my mother's voice*
and rage,   *oh god, my mother's*
frothy rage and   *voice*
time   *was gone*
along an old familiar
gravel road   *was gone*
and a dusty school-
yard i feared   *not far away*
where the soul
knows   *but gone*
there is a better place

FIELDS AND FIELDS

meandering
there is joy in the sparkling
they are and sometimes others are

stand in sparkling
        not too close
                thumping
                    always thumping
        not too close

joy   so much joy

i wait
        not too close
it's warmer and i have joy
sparkling on the ground

meandering

it's warmer

joy joy

joy

MUSING ONTARIO

within the child is a well,
an ocean where life began
and stars that land
behind every tired glance

watch her orbit a purer truth
something ancient and deep
like the water she already contains
gentle thud of waves against an aluminium hull
and this brings peace when she goes somewhere quiet
and apart

———

the most beautiful woman in the world
came to me and i knew
but could not understand
        she was a mountain
                and she was a black horse
                surging above all with dignity and
strength
and my search was over

yet there was a storm that knew no end
where nothing relents
a momentary lull in a sad inverse world

———

but it does not end
how could it?
your love is a fire most inextinguishable

let yourself feel
held in strong arms
so reliable you close your eyes

———

a tired soul alights on the other side
so a child might build new worlds in dust
        and gravel
where old gods whisper notions
and black birds explain where the good drafts are

but you already know, don't you

———

there is a dam of unnatural origin
ready to burst

take yourself to the island across the dark water
and all in real time
you will sense
the whispers and ancestors
coursing through your dreams

———

bold winds stir me into boyish frenzy
   i wake up thankful i am in one piece again
      and can fill my world with love and strength

—

in a place where a bad thing will not let go,
there will be a wave on the land
and it will wash away something very wrong
so the people on the shore can rest

then she'll remind me that beginnings
are often confounding
but they can also be the best part

DORIS (NOOKOMIS)

you could never protect them all forever
but you can love them
when the land is quiet
and the only sound
is a gentle waterfall
being heard and felt
from a different time and space

your eyes will be open to stars
and you will know they're all okay,
good mother, they always have been
and your love for them will remain
there are children in your memory
they are safe
and your love for them will remain

CURSED

there is a woman who is dead now

i don't know if she ever dies

them summon evil spirits

who don't wanna do the heavy lifting

in a water-logged barn

crooked as the woman afraid to leave

promise her she's safe as ever

and cover your ears while she screams

HOOK-LINE

he's a trap door
            that slams shut

once you've bought the ticket

            just look at it sit on a rock
    and look   it has eyes on you

            feel them somewhere in old blood
    and sometimes get   a second chance

            this time we won't see the eternity
        in the moon's cold shadow   cold
                    unlike anything i could wish
    upon beating hearts   close your eyes

                        sit on the rock and listen
                    the slithering in the deep
    is not you or i   it is not them

it is the trap door that seeks
to divide so it might fill
            its belly ...
distended
belly

TIDAL BREAK

honestly,

i don't

remember the shoreline

anymore

there's fatigue

a libido

at low tide

i boast

i make claims

but i'm swimming

out to an island

i can't see yet

horror i cannot

reckon

week five

i'm a train
you're a train
and we go

there are buffalo
galloping beside us
there is fire
fire everywhere

a pull up attack
                              hello, death
and i'm sitting in class
                                        there is a girl
and i'm not paying attention
                                                she's gone
and i wonder how
i'm supposed to be
                                i don't even know
                        what i'm doing here
but i know now

i sit in it for better or worse

and now i get to be the other one

PATRIOTS

don't open your mind to charlatans

> *a voice reciting a voice reciting*
> *something sick and wrong*

leaders don't prey on the hard-done-by
picking at their maw with cool husks

what do you really need
you won't know listening to them
their cages for children
work camps neutering a nation

> *turn 'em on each other*
> *turn 'em on the mother*

take away their relationship with the land
and they'll never know what's fighting for

i'm good for you

PANDEMIA

why are there so many bottles of water

cold, cold bottles of water

in the industrial cooler

at her majesty's disposal?

we could all probably use a good cry

people,

we don't always value the helpful release

the lights burst on

there's all the water

the orcas are coming back

the bears feel safer

crying never hurts past a certain age

holding someone would also help

week six

RED PHEASANT / MAN IN BLACK

i'm gonna walk right out of hell
i ain't trying to hurt no one
well there might be someone special,
but by now they're dead and gone
there's a line of black smoke rising
you can hear the woman screaming
and she'll always wail
cuz they took her boy
stuffed up in a big museum

my life was always my life
never had much needed less
all the ranchers ranch
the walkers walk
and the seers all born blessed
take the god up out the babies
cut the tongue out if you're to free 'em
so i bled out alone in that burned out home
lord i'd wake up but i ain't dreaming

i'm gonna walk right out of hell
i ain't never hurt no one
now my mosom walks the fields
across the bluffs into the sun
take the god up out the babies
cut the tongue up out if you're to free 'em
so i bled out alone in that burned out home
and he's off to fight koreans

there's a mother in the dark brown dirt
she wants a reason to forget
so when you hear my voice you better make a choice
or god help end up like them

when they come 'round for your children
dogs that never get their fill
take an old man's tip
put 'em in the dirt
or give your soul away piecemeal

i'm gonna walk right out of hell
i ain't trying to hurt no one
well there might be someone special
but by now they're dead and gone
there's a line of black smoke rising
you can hear the women screaming
and the fathers stand
and their lights go out
see their boys in the big museum

she has the spirit of three and will continue being remarkable for
some time   i'm happy for her, and i'm happy for them   but
for now i enjoy the quiet
                          clever books   reliable trees   the sky
she grips her push cart and wobbles around the partition
                                                        around
and around   good luck is all she knows

look up and whisper thank you for that   the wolves are just
puppies stumbling about and the water is always right for jumping in

last night i wrote a ways ahead   it was a quiet dark outside,
and the air was easy breathing   a little slower
                                                a little deeper

a movie will fly right by while you make love to the right someone
the voice on the phone relaxing you   easing the tense muscles
above your shoulders   might as well sit back and rest once
the tide starts rolling   take a look what's coming

approaching from across the hall is a tall glass of something
he places his beer bottle and plate in one hand, and uses the other
to give his lips a cursory wipe
                          "who does this guy thi—"

he takes a moment to look at you, then introduces himself with a smile
you shake hands, shake for a little while longer   he
cheerfully speaks   the particulars of what he says you are
not too particularly concerned with   but he keeps smiling, so
you keep watching him smile   and he looks in your eyes while
he tries to impress you

the two of us driving down an old gravel road   lazy
sunday morning after heavy snowfall   the cold hard
slab of bench leather not altogether unpleasant   he
seems relaxed   more focused   he wears long
johns underneath, while you've elected to forgo any un-
mentionables long or otherwise   you cite economy
of movement and steer your gaze out across all that
dormancy   he rolls those dark knowing eyes and
blasts the heat   perfectly content sipping your hot
tea, quietly admiring his fading blue jeans

    and counting down the seconds till you try again

JOHN PRINE'S REGINA

white post-its on a dull fridge
all the good news fit to print
well, i'm alive now in a good place
and i don't want what we don't get
gonna walk on out now freely
guess it be hard to accept
when the good ghosts come a calling
you wanna learn
you can't forget

old drunk uncles in the dry heat
watch 'em drive for days on end
tommy douglas, hockey sweaters,
till the herds come back again
i don't know if it gets better
when they won't see you as men
there's a bus to PA waitin'
but i won't get on again

there's a crook in every shiny seat
telling lies like good men breathe
there's a foghorn blaring 'side me
think it's time i up and leave
been an orphan with good mother
little brother and a dad
it's a long hard road to saskatoon
another indian born sad

and all my old drunk uncles
were just little boys in pain
watch 'em walk among the clouds
guess we're a little bit the same
tommy douglas on the lips here
when someone loves a little more
never told me i was missing
we don't live here anymore

week seven

WINONA

[*Addressing a modest crowd*]

really good to see you here tonight   i feel very lucky to be
here and i hope you feel some too   now, if you aren't here
for a good time, you know where the door is   and if you
bother me up here, or anyone trying to have a good time, you just
kindly raise your hand and i'll come help you find it

this song's about a girl i knew, and man, you talk about tuning
the bad out   and sometimes something that probably isn't
great for all parties concerned, can still mean everything for a
time   even while you're both staring into each other's eyes,
just waiting for the bottom to drop out

the funny thing is, if we met now, i would catch her   i would
catch her every time, and i know she'd catch me   i think she
might be one of the best lovers around, and i do mean love   so
I'm grateful for all the love and the good   when the pedal
hit the floor, we were off to the races   for a little while

and now i'm grateful for the fallout   tough as it was
because you never stop depending on the real special ones to
write about   and i'm pretty sure that big brain and that
winning smile are only getting better with time   oh, good
lord   just write a book if you're gonna yammer on

alright then   this song is called winona...

I DIED AND CAME BACK,

bet you didn't know that

                              "what did he say?"

                              "psshh, he's just drunk"

i am drunk and you can mind your own damn
business

but like I was saying, i was twenty-five years old in
1972   and let me tell you, the women?
oh man, the women!   big ones, little ones, shiny
purple sequinned rain jackets in july they'd put down
a little red carpet at the door on saturdays

saskatoon was like the new york city of the prairies,
swear to god   i don't know if tommy douglas
made saskatchewan, or saskatchewan made tommy
douglas but life was damn good

of course we didn't go to the white bars   not
much at least   unless you wanted a fight

that's just how it was

you might score a good time here and there, but who
needs the hassle?

trying to have fun and you can't stop feeling all those
eyes on you   not for me

here, have a drink

                         "christ he talks"

                         "are you cool?"

just you mind well enough   so you staying out
of trouble young blood?   you gotta remind me
to finish my story later

week eight

tipayihkewin (cree): the act of measuring or paying, or
the act of taking a measurement or dimensions; payment.

psychosis: a severe mental condition in which thought
and emotions are so affected that contact is lost with
external reality

a cousin: i remember you and i decided you spoke to________
in one of your "dreams"/"trips". he was a boy burned with
cigarettes. and living on the reserve. does that trigger
any memories for you? you said you were told that you're
a healer, or a shaman. around that time you were having
tons of dreams.

and then you told me you couldn't talk about it anymore
and told me you were not doing well. you were quite
upset at how you were feeling. i'm sorry i don't remember
anything exactly but you couldn't talk about that stuff
anymore. you had experienced psychosis and you were
seeing a therapist. you weren't sleeping.

week nine

PARTWAY BACK

learn how to manage a thousand voices
                    navigate oceans as best as you can
        them always giving you what can't be done
but the ocean can give all, and take all, quickly

        it feels right to stay on this side of the bay
but we know we gotta swim out
        some days
                some nights
we might need to go under

        i can see the basics
they're no more malevolent than my thousand voices

we're supposed to be tested
        some days
                some moments
we swim across

but we're supposed to come back

        for now at least

"what is it ever supposed to
be?"   he watches over you
with eyes floating atop drafts
not towering   how could i
explain it to you?
                    if you believed your
towers would show you god,
you'd follow them atop some-
where very high   but could you
show the ones of ages what aloft
feels like?
        i feel him watching over me when it
becomes very still   and i know there are voices
and faces are waiting, in the blood
running through their veins, creek water
sound when the bush is quiet
                    and i wonder what the eagle
sees of me   beginning to walk, to watch
mouths and lips as babes do, to create
meaning falling upward   now a simple path in
the dark
            just dreams of not mine in a sight who feels
the life and death welling in my chest   quiet water
running along between the rock i would walk and
step upon

AGOOJIN

she's gonna fly a country wide

    one day chasing

    next day running

        all around the world

     like we used to

place a kiss on the back of my neck   the coffee is still hot   steam gently
          rising   and we leave the patio door open   men finishing off
                    a new building,   groan and hiss of bus lines
                              writing again   feeling bigger
                                   need a reason to put
                                        my pen down
                                          for a little
                                            while

SNOW MELTING ON YOUR PARENTS' DRIVEWAY

stay in it

                   somewhere you know it's special

                  don't worry about time

               somewhere you know it's snow melting

on your parents' driveway

                the girls are women with responsibilities

       but they're still girls and they like that you're still a boy

                     don't mind that you're a man

and you don't know enough to worry anyways

       you can feel the drums

        now you know they never stop

               it never stops beating

         none of it

       you're meant to change

and that's okay

             the drums keep beating

stay in it

be special

week ten

GREGOR HARBOUR

i know the rules
i've been playing too long
if i needed love, darling,
i expect i'd be gone

waking up with the spirit,
lord, i still feel alone
now the deed's in my name
and it won't change
but this don't feel like home

i'm pulling my boat cross the rocks out of old gregor harbour
gonna make up a supper once i put this old boat away
but i know she'll have a dull moment
and she'll come a calling
and i'll push off tomorrow
but i won't find the great hudson bay

she's a peach
she's a bear
well, they broke all the rules with that mouth
and that pretty black hair

and the ones that have once died and gone
are still laughing
and they dance while the radio's on
but i still love this side of macgregor
even if it ain't fair

i'm pulling my boat cross the rocks out of old gregor harbour
got a plate in the fridge once i put this old boat away
but i know she'll have a dull moment
and she'll come a calling
and i'll push off tomorrow
but i won't find the great hudson bay

STRING CORRAL

the string sways

 and the grass swells

 and recedes

you build your temporary so high

 never think to go under

it's okay to be afraid

 you go down a little ways

and you see different

 talk better

a lot of mothers are singing

and now the worst is over

week eleven

cold water and my heavy shorts clung to my skinny
legs   and every open beer bottle was accounted for
          what's the deal with heaven if the holy spirit
already exists in all of us?

                              questions and double-talk
          the uncles holding their drinks a little tighter
when i'm around   half-buried already in the dark
soil below the weathered balcony   the dark soil up
from the beach along the shore in the shadowy trees
          where i was born   where i'll go again in time

the flowers peered upward in groups of sleepy threes
beside my empty hands and the hungry hole in my
heart   the way there was supposed to be another
one of us burning in our mother's mind like bright
spirits waiting across the bay with open arms

                                        maybe i
was just the child   alive and well on the shore near
the shadowy trees   peering across water at the
little pyres burning bright in the distance and bright
at my feet

week twelve

BRIGHT EYES

no one burst through the surface
but that doesn't mean they weren't

the boys sure noticed
and so did you

what have you always known
    deep down
        somewhere clear?

the important lies you told
aren't even lies laying down tonight

it's scary

but what did you really see?

CHURCH AND SEIZURE

faint

when they came for me

the world became awfully quiet

a lifetime waiting

on thrashing

and tooth and nail

but it goes the other way

complied without complaining

and the desperation

was a final breath

breaching the surface

at a crowded beach

i was bred to slip away quietly

in a nightmare upon awakening

NEPHEW ON THE WAY

when the stars shone

  in their eyes and my heart

when the stars shone through their eyes

      and my simple heart

    skipped along its brightest beat

and mothers and fathers lost years

    and took on new meaning

water makes its way across

        a cosmos painted long ago

   spirits warm and glow like ember light

within the circle

  an older man

    smiles with joy in his heart

   maybe he never lets on all he saw coming

RODNEY EVERETT (SEVEN GENERATIONS)

i could never speak like generations ago
and tell you it was all true

but sleep easy knowing it was no lie

babies were born
and the river flowed along as ever

yet the crooked would cast your eyes away

you were designed to rest
to sleep
to dream
do not allow the most unnatural
to steer your gaze
to close your eyes

join hand in hand
with brother and sisters
seven generations will see what you see

consider what they know

week thirteen

SHORT THOUGHTS ON TOXIC WHITE

the thing is

i do know some truths

no boatload could carry them off

somewhere remote and dull

where blind dogs lose their words

fear their own sisters

and poison what would be of them

IN MEMORIAM

    walking along the brushline

even a warm group of four

    could spook a child

        voices that aren't

           really there,

    but mean so much more

on our back in the sun,

    you're just as blind to it all now

      as you ever were

holding up a candle to change the metre

DROWNING LESSONS (RED DEER, AB)

it's spending decades

    standing outside the party

        watching pretty girls get into cars for the night

        playing games to stay away from

rope and poison

        live here

      you write among stars

      you know what it is to walk falling upward

       and growing healthier all the time

mind you don't swim in water that was not there

DRIFT

if i could take off my shirt and lie down
beside you   wrap my arms around
your chest and waist   and pull us
firmly together   you could know
what safe feels like, and let go unto me
        pressing your hips back into good
warm exhalation on your naked ear and
the back of your bare neck   good
        pressure   desperate fingertips
and a large hand gently guiding your
throat in a new direction   welcome
alarms ringing out   old hurts fading
away   the reassuring inevitability of
a cycle dictated by a star of unknown
origin   and a man dangerously close
and underside of something very soft and
needful   pushing against you and
then   *stars*   bright lights begin
to soften   a current runs somewhere
deeper   where a tired lust is ache like
ancient waves smashing creation against
the rock   *the pounding*   *the*
ocean   over and over   again,
again   thunder of your own making
        fingernails leaving expressions of
ownership   and bared teeth pressed
into the welcome flesh of one who seeks
to protect and destroy   whimpers and
cries build, build into a place bereft of
sound and thought   where the rock
yields identity and becomes the wave

        and the waters would run above,
below, through new ground   over
and over   again, again   until
explosions subside   *souls mended*
anew   into gentle give   and
gentle   take   his chest rising and
falling slowly in time with your own
measured breath   lazy, deft fingers
slowly working through tousled hair
and the memory of salty mist you feel on
skin and taste on soft parted lips
        long after drifting off together in a
safe place

HERE TO THERE

i woke wondering,

    what will become

of what I know?

                for time was I

        the ghost of another

and my mind would swim out

      and float up   again, again

    untethered like a calf of summer

        but what watches?

and how it feels to wash away

   carrying me down

   falling through clouds   and then more

  my mother and father are peace

      and I was not ready to forget it all

NOTES / GLOSSARY

p.3	mikisiw-wacîk	eagle hills	cree
p.10	okâwîmâ	mother	cree
p.12, 65	mosom	grandfather	cree
p.12	nohkom	grandmother	cree
p.14	mississippi	great river	cree oji
p.15	nimishoomis	my grandfather	ojibwe
p.49	giizhig	sky, heaven, or day	ojibwe
p.53	nookomis	my grandmother	ojibwe
p.85	agoojin	she hangs in the sky	ojibwe

ACKNOWLEDGMENTS

My family, who have always been strong for me when I was not able to carry myself. Indinawemaaganidog (all my relations in ojibwe).

Sarain Stump, Brenda M. Knight, Lisa Monita, Monica Sommerville, Claire Kelly, Emory Wells, Teresa Wong, Andrey and Nina Schmidt, A.J. Devlin, Marsha Smith, Allen Sapp, Eric Forbes and family, The Dieter family, Sage Zobell, Margot Hurlbert, Markiel and Raquel Simpson, Linda Jane, JD Sallinger, William Faulkner, John Steinbeck, Larry McMurtry, Cormac McCarthy, Charles Bukowski, Bill Watterson, John Prine, Townes Van Zandt, Katie Crutchfield, James Baldwin, and Sam Shepard.

In 2017, to honour NeWest Press' 40th anniversary, we inaugurated a new poetry series to go alongside our Nunatak First Fiction, Prairie Play, and Writer as Critic series: Crow Said Poetry. Crow Said is named in honour of Robert Kroetsch's foundational 1977 novel *What The Crow Said.* The series aims to shed light on places and people outside of the literary mainstream. It is our intention that the poets featured in this series will continue Robert Kroetsch's literary tradition of innovation, interrogation, and generosity of spirit.

CROW SAID POETRY TITLES AVAILABLE FROM NEWEST

Tar Swan — David Martin

That Light Feeling Under Your Feet — Kayla Geitzler

Paper Caskets — Emilia Danielewska

let us not think of them as barbarians — Peter Midgley

Lullabies in the Real World — Meredith Quartermain

The Response of Weeds: A Misplacement of Black Poetry on the Prairies — Bertrand Bickersteth

Coconut — Nisha Patel

rump + flank — Carol Harvey Steski

How to Hold a Pebble — Jaspreet Singh

Kink Bands — David Martin

Attic Rain — Samantha Jones

Dreams of the Epoch & the Rock — Jaspreet Singh

The Beauty of Vultures — Wendy McGrath & Danny Miles

All Wrong Horses on Fire That Go Away in the Rain — Sarain Frank Soonias

SARAIN FRANK SOONIAS is Cree and Ojibwe.
He began writing poetry in 2020, and now focuses
on acting and playwriting. His poetry collection
*ALL WRONG HORSES ON FIRE THAT GO AWAY IN
THE RAIN* was written over five months during a
severe breakdown while attending therapy through
a TRC initiative for children and grandchildren
of Residential School and Sixties Scoop survivors.
He believes that the notion of colonization is
poisonous for all concerned parties.